Brimming with creative inspiration, how-to projects, and useful information to enrich your everyday life, Quarto Knows is a favorite destination for those pursuing their interests and passions. Visit our site and dig deeper with our books into your area of interest: Quarto Creates, Quarto Cooks, Quarto Homes, Quarto Lives, Quarto Drives, Quarto Explores, Quarto Gifts, or Quarto Kids.

First Published in 2017 by Walter Foster Jr., an imprint of The Quarto Group.
6 Orchard Road, Suite 100, Lake Forest, CA 92630, USA.
T (949) 380-7510 F (949) 380-7575 www.QuartoKnows.com

Walter Foster Jr. titles are also available at discount for retail, wholesale, promotional, and bulk purchase. For details, contact the Special Sales Manager by email at specialsales@quarto.com or by mail at The Quarto Group, Attn: Special Sales Manager, 401 Second Avenue North, Suite 310, Minneapolis, MN 55401 USA.

ISBN: 978-1-63322-396-7

Written by Joe Rhatigan
Illustrated by Lisa Perrett

Printed in China
10 9 8 7 6 5 4 3 2 1

MIX
Paper from responsible sources
FSC® C104723

50

WACKY THINGS
HUMANS DO

Weird and amazing facts about the human body!

Written by Joe Rhatigan
Illustrated by Lisa Perrett

Walter Foster
Jr.

TABLE OF CONTENTS

YOUR BIZARRE BODY

Which of the following
do you think your body
is doing right this minute?
- Glowing
- Smelling
- Sweating
- Rumbling
- Tingling
- Shedding

If you guessed "all of the above," you're absolutely right.

Your body also wrinkles, bends, twists, sneezes,
burps, yawns, and giggles. And this book will tell
you why and how your body does all these things and more.

You will be amazed, dazed, and maybe
even a little alarmed. But don't worry!
No matter how incredible
these body facts may seem,
they're all perfectly normal.
Yes, your body is weird and wacky,
but so is everybody else's!

NO. 1
RAISIN FINGERS

The next time you take a long bath or spend a lot of time in a pool, take a look at your fingers. They'll be wrinkled like raisins. Same goes for your toes. It's nothing to worry about—wrinkly fingers and toes happen to just about everybody. But why? Is water getting under your skin, making it soggy? Nope! Your body's nervous system—the part of your body that controls your actions—is constricting, or making narrower, the blood vessels just below the skin. This causes your fingers and toes to wrinkle.

MORE ABOUT WRINKLY DIGITS

If your body is making your fingers wrinkle, there must be a good reason for it. Scientists have recently discovered that wrinkly fingers are better than dry fingers at picking up wet objects. The wrinkles also help your toes get a better grip when walking on wet surfaces. They channel away the water like the treads on a car tire.

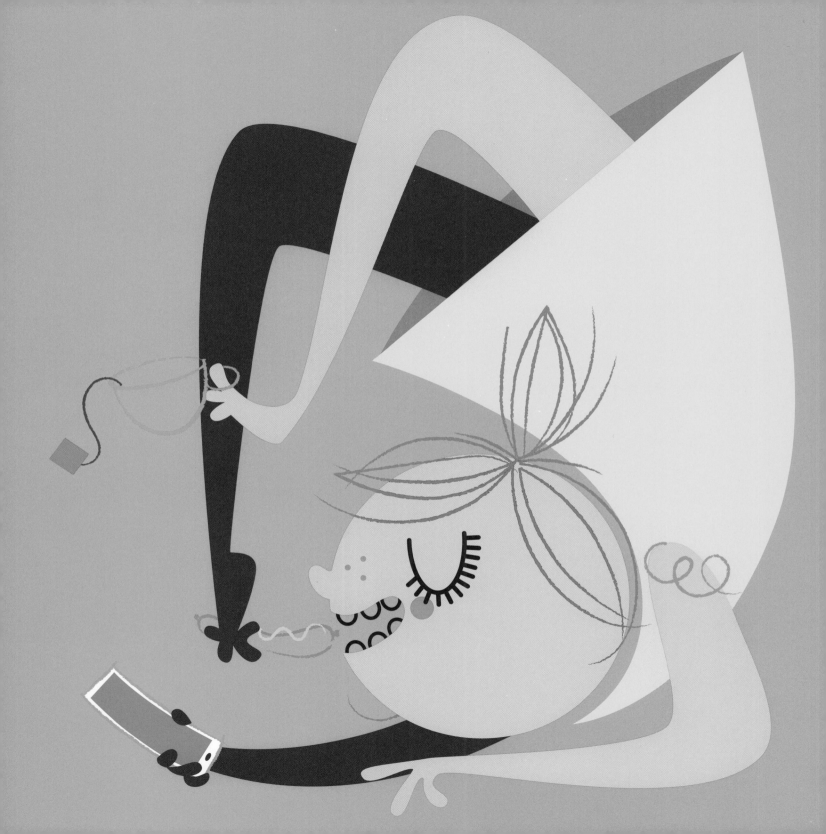

NO. 2
BENDY BODIES

Some people—around 20 percent—can bend over backward, lay their hands on the floor without bending their knees, place their feet behind their heads, and more. These people are double-jointed, although they have the same number of joints as everybody else. Joints are the points in the body where two bones meet. The elbows, knees, wrists, and knuckles are examples of joints. Double-jointed people can move a bone within a joint a lot more than the rest of us. This makes them very flexible. And even though it looks like it hurts, it doesn't.

MORE ABOUT PRETZEL PEOPLE

Contortionists are people who can bend, twist, and flex their bodies into shapes or positions that look impossible. Most contortionists are born very flexible, but a lot of training and practice also goes into being able to turn yourself into a human pretzel!

NO. 3
SHINE BRIGHT

Your body gives off light, much like a firefly or a glow worm—or a superhero. Sadly, nobody can see it. Using special cameras, scientists have proven that our bodies glow. The light is so weak, however, that our eyes would have to be one thousand times stronger to see it. Most of the light comes from our foreheads, cheeks, and necks. This glow is a result of chemical reactions in our bodies that give off small particles of light. The light brightens and fades throughout the day, with the most light produced in the middle of the afternoon. Even though you can't see this light, it's pretty awesome knowing it's there.

MORE ABOUT GLOWING

There are several animals that produce visible light, including fireflies, jellyfish, glow worms, and some species of fish and deep-sea dwellers. This is called *bioluminescence*. Animals use this light to attract mates, lure prey, defend against predators, and communicate.

NO. 4
SNIFF TIME MACHINE

The king is walking back to the palace from his daily jaunt and catches a whiff of some flowers in the garden. He thinks, "Hey, these are the same flowers that I used to give to the queen twenty years ago, before she was turned into a frog." What!? How can he remember that? Your sense of smell can trigger really strong emotions and memories—much more so than your other senses. That's because smells are processed by the same part of the brain that deals with emotion and memory. This can lead to feeling like you're traveling back in time.

MORE ABOUT NOSES

Your nose—well, actually, it's your brain—can recall more than 50,000 smells, even if you haven't smelled them in years. It can also smell up to 1 trillion different odors, making it the most sensitive organ in the body.

NO. 5
SEEING, NOT ALWAYS BELIEVING

Our brains do everything for us, but we can't always rely on them. For example, look closely at the image on the opposite page. It's a weird-looking face. But what happens if you flip it upside down? Something (or someone) that you didn't see before is there. This is called an *optical illusion*. Some optical illusions even look like they're moving if you stare at them long enough—even though you know it's impossible for an image to move! Basically, your brain is lying to you. Bad brain!

MORE ABOUT OPTICAL ILLUSIONS

When you go to the movies, your brain is being fooled in two important ways. First, when you watch actors talking, you think the sound is coming from their mouths, but it's actually coming from speakers in the theater. Second, nothing is really moving, except a bunch of still photographs on a reel of film—like a hi-tech flip book!

NO. 6
SUPER STRENGTH & SPEED

There are many true tales of people gaining super strength in times of danger, such as someone lifting a car to save a loved one trapped underneath. While scientists don't really believe anyone can lift a car, your body can get stronger and faster in high-pressure situations. When you experience fear, a chemical called *adrenaline* is released into your bloodstream. It makes your heart beat faster, increases breathing capacity, and shuts down other bodily functions. This lets your muscles concentrate on running faster than you ever thought possible or using strength you didn't know you had.

MORE ABOUT SUPER POWERS

News stories about normal people performing with superhero strength include a woman who fought off a polar bear, a man who lifted a crashed helicopter, two teenage girls who lifted a tractor to save their father, and a man who bent a burning car's door in half to save the people inside.

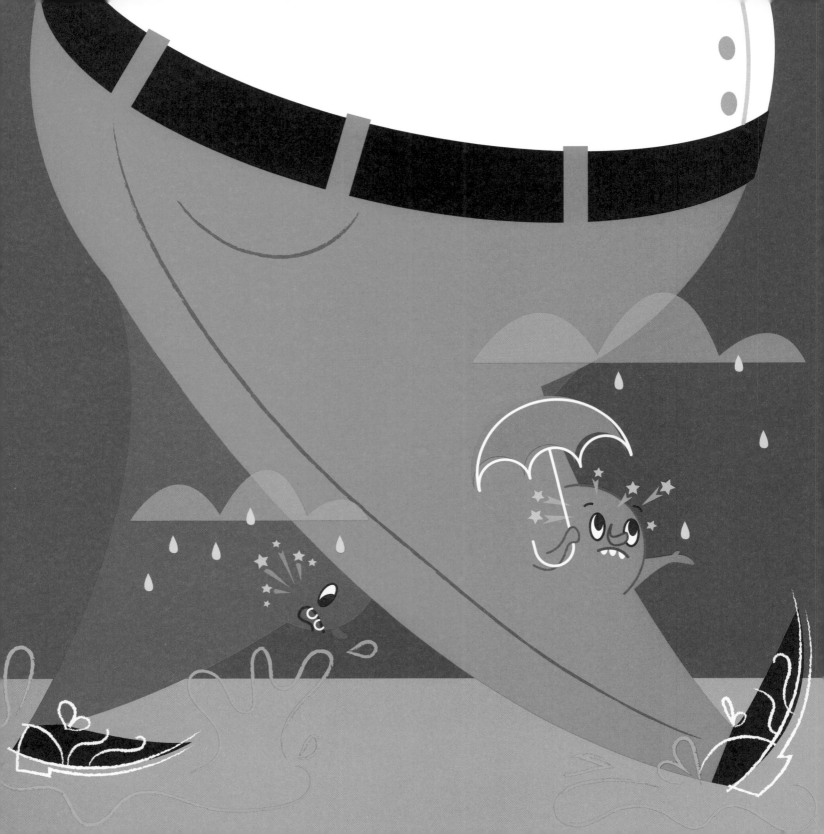

NO. 7
RAIN CAUSES PAIN

It's a beautiful, sunny day, but your great-uncle Bill is complaining. "Oh, my knee is aching. It's going to rain tomorrow for sure." The next day, it does! Scientists believe that our bodies, especially joints that already experience some pain, can predict the weather. When bad weather begins to roll in, the barometric pressure around us lowers. This gives the tissues surrounding joints a little more room to expand, which puts more pressure on the joints and causes pain.

MORE ABOUT JOINTS & WEATHER

Barometric pressure is the weight of the air that surrounds us. It pushes against our skin, even though we don't feel it. Most people think it's the damp, cold weather that causes the joint pain, but it's actually the change in air pressure.

NO. 8
VOLUME CONTROL

Have you ever wondered why someone screaming at you hurts your ears but your own screaming doesn't? When you're about to talk, sing, or yell, muscles in your ears contract in order to reduce or lessen whatever noise is about to come out of your mouth. (These muscles also help to lower the sound of your own chewing.) So you can karaoke at the top of your lungs and your ears will be just fine.

MORE ABOUT HEARING

If you want to hear your own voice (or chewing) louder, stick your fingers loosely in your ears. Sound vibrations will bounce off your fingers and head back into the eardrum, which will give your voice a booming or echo-like sound. Try it!

NO. 9
HA, HA HEALTHY

The next time you're not feeling so well, try this simple experiment: start laughing. Find a funny video or a silly book and giggle and guffaw for a while. According to scientific studies, laughter truly is the best medicine. Laughing lowers stress, reduces pain, puts you in a good mood, and protects your heart from disease. Some cancer treatment centers even offer laughter therapy for their patients.

MORE ABOUT LAUGHING

Babies begin laughing at around four months old—long before language develops. Laughing is an unconscious behavior, which means we don't decide to do it. It just happens. This is why it's often easy to tell if someone is fake laughing. Laughing is also social (we don't laugh as often when we're alone), and, best of all, contagious!

NO. 10
SPEEDY SNEEZE

Ah...Ah...Ah...CHOOOO! That's the sound of your nose rocketing out a germ-y spray of gunk at speeds of up to 100 miles per hour. A sneeze is your nose's powerful way of getting rid of dust, pollen, animal dander, pollutants, or anything else that doesn't belong up there. Not only does a sneeze get rid of that stuff quickly, but it also sends it far—not quite into outer space, but up to 200 feet away! Unless you're covering your mouth—as you should!

MORE ON SNEEZES

Sneezes often come in pairs or groups of three. That's because it usually takes more than one sneeze to get rid of whatever's bothering the nose. The world record for the most sneezes in a row belongs to a woman in England who sneezed for 977 days without stopping.

NO. 11
RUMP RUMBLES

Our wonderful bodies sometimes make not-so-wonderful noises. Some of these noises are followed up by even worse smells. That's right, our bodies produce gas. Everything we eat and drink gives us gas, and in a normal day, you probably pass gas anywhere from 14 to 20 times—producing enough gas to fill a party balloon. That's one balloon you wouldn't want to pop!

MORE ON STINKY SOUNDS

The noise comes from the gas leaving your rear end. The smell comes from colonies of bacteria in the lower intestinal tract. While turning food into nutrients, the bacteria produce hydrogen sulfide gas, which stinks like rotten eggs. Sugary foods such as milk, fruit, and beans produce the most gas. Meanwhile, cauliflower, meat, and eggs usually produce the stinkiest smells.

NO. 12
ALL TRESSED UP

Rapunzel is a fairy tale for a reason. First, nobody could grow hair that long. Second, as soon as the prince climbed her hair, Rapunzel would likely fall out of the window because her neck muscles wouldn't be strong enough to support his weight. One thing is true however: Rapunzel's tresses would definitely be strong enough to hold the prince. In fact, each of our hair strands could support the weight of a candy bar. So, if you have 100,000 strands of hair, which is about the average number per person, that would be enough to support a couple of elephants.

MORE HAIR-MAZING FACTS

The reason your hair clogs up your pipes in the bathroom is that it is nearly indestructible. It decays very slowly and cannot be destroyed by cold temperatures, water, or even many chemicals.

NO. 13
LIFT IT, BABY!

If you think babies are soft, cuddly blobs of weakness, think again. For all their tininess, babies have really powerful legs. For instance, if a baby were the size of an ox, it would be more than able to pull a cart. That's not all—a newborn's grip is so strong that if a baby grabbed hold of your finger, you could lift the baby up in the air, and it wouldn't let go. But don't try that with your little siblings!

MORE ABOUT BABY SUPERPOWERS

Up until around 6 months in age, babies are capable of moving around underwater with their eyes and mouth open. Their windpipe automatically closes, and they can spend a short time underwater. But don't test this with your little siblings either!

NO. 14
BODY HEAT

In order to move, our bodies need energy, which we get from food. The process of breaking down food releases the necessary energy, as well as extra energy in the form of heat. The body doesn't need this extra heat energy, so it gets rid of it through the skin. This heat may not seem like much, but if you could capture it, you could use it to boil water or power a light bulb.

MORE ON HUMAN HEAT

In the not-so-distant future, you may be able to charge your smartphone or run a laptop from energy converted from your own body heat. Several inventions are in the works to use our bodies as batteries for our devices. So instead of plugging into a wall socket, you'd plug into yourself.

NO. 15
PINS & NEEDLES

You see a ball coming your way. Your eyes send a message to your brain, which in turn, sends another message to your arms and hands to catch the ball. Your body is full of nerve pathways and blood vessels that help send these messages. However, if you sit cross-legged too long or if you lean on your arm in a funny way, you can block these pathways— sort of like when you step on a garden hose and the water won't come out. This causes your limb to "fall asleep" and feel numb.

MORE ON SLEEPING LIMBS

When you shake your asleep arm or leg, or change positions, blood flows back into the cut-off areas, causing a tingly pain that hurts until everything goes back to normal.

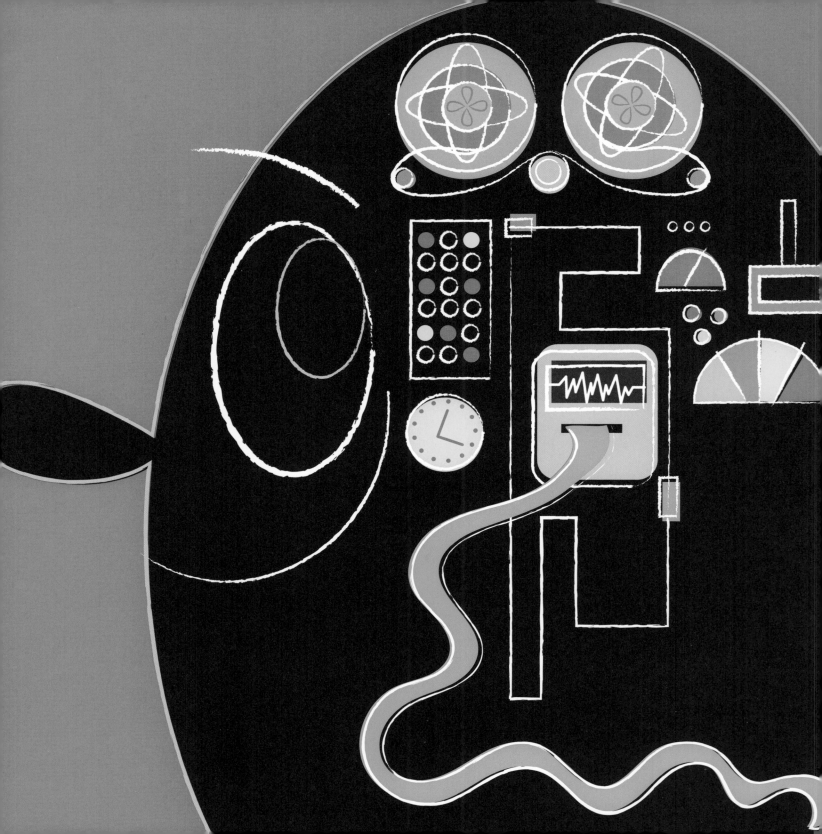

NO. 16
BRAIN SCIENCE

Computers can beat human chess champions, poker experts, and even quiz show brainiacs. But did you know your brain can perform 38 quadrillion operations per second (or 38,000,000,000,000,000)? When scientists wanted to imitate one second of a normal brain's activity, they needed 82,000 computers. And while the smartest computers out there need enough electricity to power up to 10,000 homes, your brain operates on the amount of energy it would take to turn on a dim light bulb.

MORE ABOUT BRAINS

Our brains can still do many things better than computers, such as solving crossword puzzles, creating art, writing, and recognizing faces.

NO. 17
GIMME SOME SKIN!

Your skin covers your entire body and accounts for 16 percent of your body weight. It's also responsible for a whole bunch of dust around your home. That's because you shed—just like a dog or cat—up to 500 million cells every day! Dead skin falls off and is replaced by new skin. In fact, every month you have an all-new outer layer of skin. And in a lifetime, you will have shed around 100 pounds of skin.

MORE ABOUT YOUR SKIN

The outer layer of skin is called the *epidermis*, and is composed of cells made of *keratin*, a hard substance that also forms your hair and nails. This layer protects the cells below it from bacteria and infection, poisons, and sunlight.

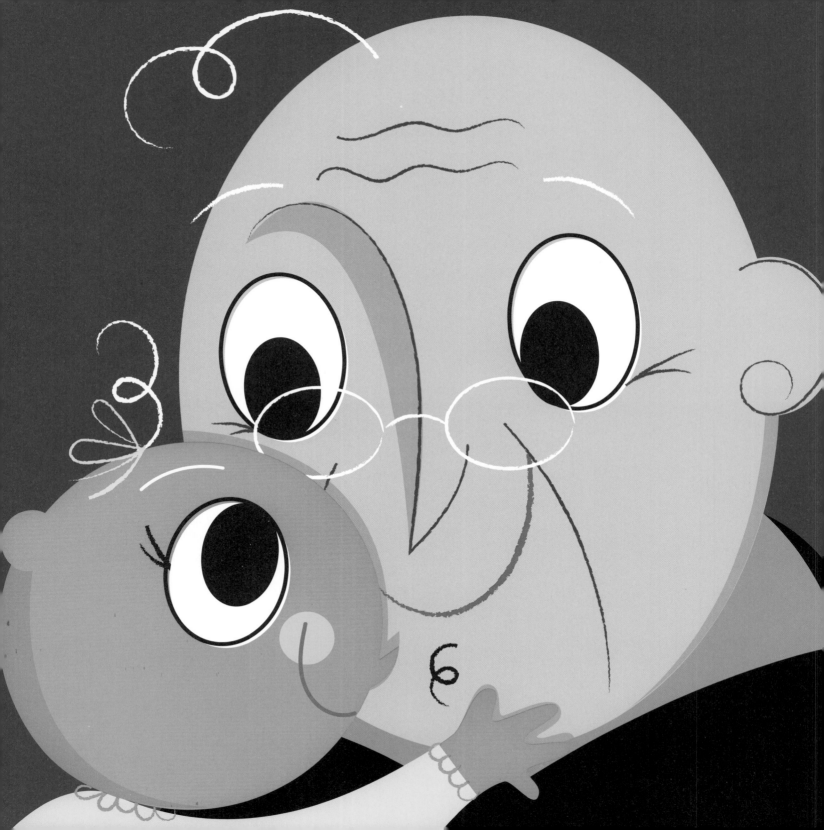

NO. 18
BABY FACE

There's one thing babies are really good at: looking cute. A lot of that cuteness comes from their giant eyes. At birth, a baby's eyes are already nearly the size they will be for the rest of the baby's life. Scientists who study cuteness (yes, there are scientists that study cuteness!) note that adults prefer babies with big eyes. Maybe that's why babies get so much attention!

MORE ON FACES

The rest of the baby's facial features play catch-up to the eyes. For a long time, people believed the ears and nose kept growing until old age. But while these features do appear to change over time, they are not actually growing, just drooping and sagging because of gravity!

NO. 19
TONGUE TRICKS

Your tongue helps you chew, swallow, talk, sing, and of course, taste your food. The rest of the time, it's just hanging around in your mouth. Maybe that's why people try these simple tongue tricks. Can you touch the tip of your nose with your tongue? If so, you are one of around 10 percent of people with this special skill. Can you lick your elbow? Only a few people have a long enough tongue and a short enough arm. These tricks don't take any special skills—just the right-sized body parts. Here's one you can practice: fold your tongue in half.

MORE BODY TRICKS

Here are some other tricks to try when you're bored: raise one eyebrow, wink, twitch your nose, and wiggle your ears (see page 69). If you can't do them, don't give up! You can train your body to do many of these. All it takes is practice.

NO. 20
SNOT'S AMAZING

Boogers don't just happen. Your incredible body makes snot on purpose for a very important reason. Whether green and gooey or white and crusty, snot clogs up your nostrils in order to trap dangerous viruses and keep them from attacking through the holes in your nose. Once the snot has captured the bad stuff, it will kill the invaders. All you have to do is blow. That's yet another wonderful reason to stop picking your nose!

MORE ON MUCUS

Boogers and snot are also called *mucus*, and you produce 1 to 2 pints (.5 to .9 L) of it a day. This sticky substance does more than defend. Your mouth, nose, throat, lungs, and other parts produce mucus to keep these parts of your body moist. Otherwise they'll dry out and crack. Ouch!

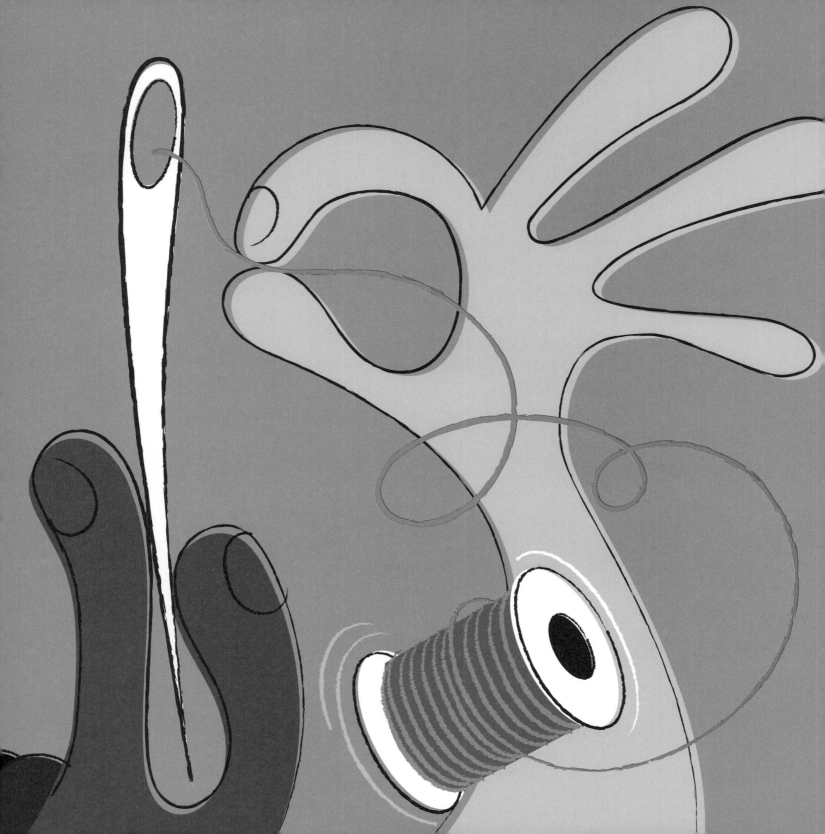

NO. 21
TOUCHY FEELY

Your fingers are fabulous at grabbing, flicking, pointing, poking, and picking. Most impressive, however, is a finger's ability to feel. The fingers are just about the most sensitive parts of your body. This is due to the large number of *nerve endings*, or receptors that send your brain information about the outside world. Your fingers are so sensitive that they can feel the tiniest piece of thread or a piece of hair on the table that has been split lengthwise four times. Your eyes may not even be able to see these hair pieces, but your fingers can feel them.

MORE FASCINATING FINGER FACTS

Fingers are sensitive to temperature, texture, moisture, pressure, and vibration. Fingernails grow an average of 1/10 of an inch (3 millimeters) per month, although children's nails grow faster than adults'.

NO. 22
BRRRAIN

The double chocolate ice cream tastes delicious—but suddenly a lightning bolt of pain jabs you in the brain. What in the world just happened? A scientist might say you are suffering from *sphenopalatine ganglioneuralgia*. But don't worry—that's just a fancy way of saying you have an ice cream headache or brain freeze. When cold food or drink hits the roof of the mouth, blood vessels swell and tighten quickly, causing pain in the brain. It usually goes away within 30 seconds.

MORE ON BRAIN FREEZE

There are lots of ways to stop brain freeze. Try pressing your tongue against the roof of your mouth or drinking something warm. The heat and pressure may help. If that doesn't work, cover your open mouth with your hand, and then breathe in through your mouth and out through your nose. The best cure is to eat your ice cream slowly!

NO. 23
FUNKY FEET

If you have stinky feet, you're not alone. Our feet get foul because they sweat—a lot! Each foot has around 250,000 sweat glands and can produce a cup of sweat a day. The sweat itself doesn't smell—it's mostly water, salt, and potassium—but the bacteria on your feet eat the sweat and produce foul-smelling waste. Want your feet to smell more like flowers? Keep them dry!

MORE ABOUT SWEAT

Sweat glands secrete sweat in order to cool us down and keep our body temperature normal. That's why we sweat when we are hot. The moisture evaporates and cools us off a little. Sweat glands are found all over our body, but feet have a lot more than other body parts.

NO. 24
HEIGHT ADJUSTMENTS

If you measure yourself first thing in the morning and again just before bedtime, you might notice that you're shorter at night. That's because your body shrinks throughout the day—you could lose up to ½ inch (1.27 cm) of height. Your spine has 23 jelly-like discs that act like shock absorbers for when you're jumping, running, or even just standing. These discs are made mostly of water, which gets squished and squeezed, leaving you shorter than you were when you first woke up. A good night's sleep restores you to your regular height.

MORE ON SPINE STRETCHING

Gravity is the force that compresses our spine throughout the day. So what happens to astronauts who don't have gravity to deal with? They gain up to two inches of height in space!

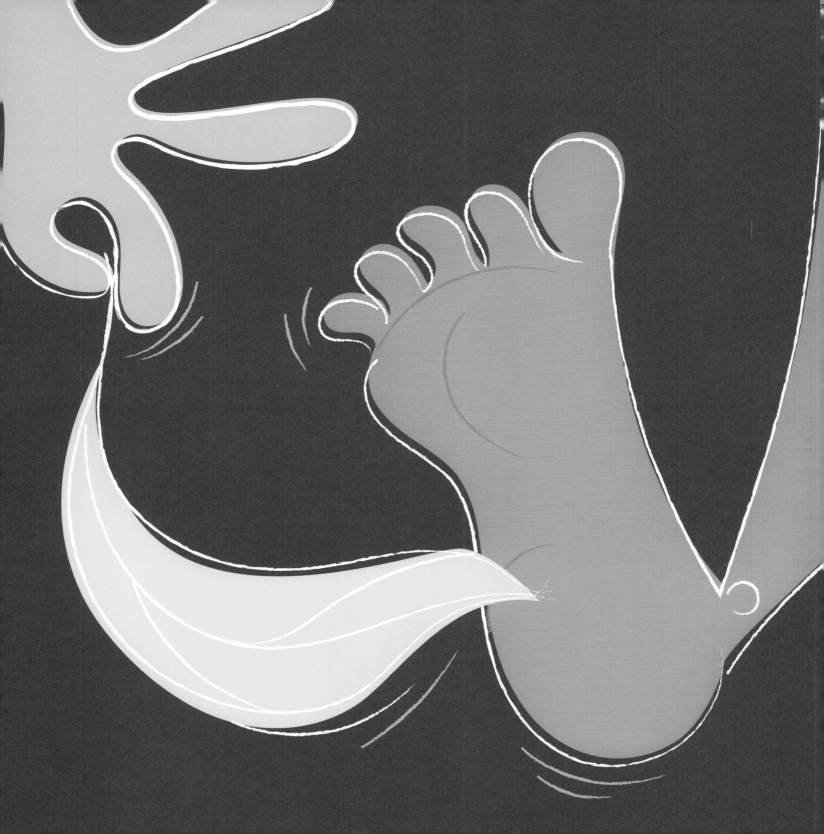

NO. 25
TICKLE, TICKLE

Are your feet ticklish? How about your neck or armpits? When a friend lightly touches you with a finger or a feather, your brain sends what's called a *tickle response*, making you giggle and jerk around. Scientists believe tickling promotes human bonding (which is why we love to tickle babies), as well as acts as an alarm system for critters crawling on our skin. If the brain knows where and how the tickling will happen, there won't be a tickle response. That's why you can't tickle yourself!

MORE ON TICKLING

The next time someone tries to tickle you, place your hands over theirs as they tickle. This gives your brain more information about the tickling and won't send out the tickle response. See if it works!

NO. 26
YOU SMELL

You smell. I smell. We all smell! And we all smell different. Some of us smell like roses, and others like stinky socks. Our body odor is like a fingerprint—no two odor types are the same, and we can be identified by our smell. Your unique body odor comes from the different combinations of molecules in your sweat and other bodily fluids that travel through the air. Scientists have done tests that show that we can pick out our own scent.

MORE ON ODORS
Dogs have a better sense of smell than us. Not only can dogs identify their human family members by their smells, but some also have been trained to smell cancer in humans!

NO. 27
CAMERA EYES

The next time you take a picture with a camera, think about this: Your eyes work a lot like the camera does! When you snap a picture, light passes through the lens and is sent upside down to the sensor to be captured and saved by the camera's memory. Your camera adjusts the image so you see it right-side up. Similarly, when light passes through your eye, your iris *dilates*, or expands, to help the lens focus the light and send the image to the retina at the back of your eye. At this point, the image is also upside down. The retina sends the upside-down picture to your brain as an electrical signal. Your brain flips the picture right-side up so you don't get confused!

MORE ON UPSIDE-DOWN VISION
Humans can process images in 13/1000 of a second. These images start upside down because the cornea, where light enters the eye, is curved. The image received by the retina at the back of the eye looks like the reflection of your face from the front of a spoon.

NO. 28
MAGIC BODY TRICKS

Stand inside a doorframe and press the backs of your hands against the frame for 30 seconds, as if you're trying to push the frame outward. Then let your arms down and step away from the doorframe. Your arms will "magically" float upward. Scientists call this the *Kohnstamm phenomenon*, and it's not really magic. Basically, the part of your brain responsible for your limbs gets fooled easily, and it thinks your arms are still pushing against the frame.

MORE MAGIC TRICKS

Have a friend sit in front of you in a chair. Close your eyes. Reach around and place one hand on their nose. At the same time, put your other hand on your own nose. Stroke both noses. After about a minute, your brain will jump to the conclusion that your nose has grown to be extremely long.

NO. 29
BLACK-AND-BLUE

You banged your leg on a ladder. Ouch! You got hit in the eye by a baseball (or a boxing glove!). Double ouch! Anytime your body gets banged up, there's a chance your skin will do something amazing—it will change colors. That's because even though the bump you got didn't break the skin, it did break a bunch of little veins right under the skin. This releases red blood cells around the area where you got hurt, which changes your skin to a dark black-and-blue or purple color.

MORE ABOUT BRUISES

Red blood cells are part of your blood. If you look at them under a microscope, they look like flattened dodgeballs. They help carry oxygen to your brain and remove carbon dioxide from your body. Once they surround your bruise, the red blood cells die and turn darker in color, which is why your bruise changes colors as well.

NO. 30
TUMMY TALKS

You walk into the ice cream store and you can see and smell all the amazing treats inside. Suddenly a strange grumbling, rumbling, growling noise comes from your stomach. It's loud, long, and a little embarrassing. Many people will hear their stomachs rumble and say, "I'm just hungry." That's not why your stomach is making noises though. That sound indicates that your digestive system is moving food and gas along through your intestines. The sound is louder because there isn't anything in there to muffle the noise.

MORE ON INTESTINES

The small intestine is a long tube that absorbs most of the nutrients and minerals from your food. It's between the stomach and the large intestines and can be up to 25 feet (7.6 m) long.

NO. 31
HAIR-RAISING GOOSEBUMPS

Did you ever dip a toe in the water only to get the chills? Whenever we get cold or feel strong emotions (fear or surprise for example), tiny muscles around the hairs on our body automatically contract, or tighten. This causes the little hairs we have on our bodies to stand on end, creating *goosebumps*. They are called goosebumps because our skin looks like a plucked goose.

MORE ON GOOSEBUMPS

In humans, goosebumps are a *vestigial response*, or a leftover response from a time when we had layers of hair all over our bodies. Goosebumps help furry animals stay warm. When their hair is raised, it traps a layer of air around the skin—keeping the skin warm.

NO. 32
WE HIC...HIC... HICCUP

Your pizza is so good that you eat it as quickly as you can. Then you follow it up with three quick gulps from your soda. Before you can grab another slice though, you begin making a strange, uncontrollable sound. "Hic...hic...hic." You have the hiccups! Feel free to blame your *diaphragm*, a muscle at the bottom of your chest that helps you with your breathing. When it gets bothered (eating and drinking too quickly will bother your diaphragm), it forces air out of your lungs in such a way that you can't help but hiccup.

STOP THOSE HICCUPS!

There are many ways people try to get rid of hiccups, including: holding their breath, drinking water quickly, biting on a lemon, gargling with water, pulling their tongue, and breathing slowly. The most popular way is to have someone scare the hiccups away. Does that work for you? Boo!

NO. 33
WIGGLY EARS

Not everyone can do it, but some humans can wiggle their ears. This is what's called a *vestigial response*. That means ear wiggling was once important for humans to be able to do, but is no longer needed. (See "Hair-Raising Goosebumps" on page 65.) Long ago, ear wiggling helped early humans listen for predators or prey. Now we only do it because it makes people laugh.

EARS SOMETHING INTERESTING
Those strange and interesting twists, folds, and lobes on your ear aren't just there to look funny. They help collect, amplify, and direct sound waves to the ear canal. And they're just right for capturing what we most need to hear: other human voices.

NO. 34
FOOT RACE

Cheetahs are the fastest land animal on earth. They can run up to 60 miles per hour (97 kmh), which is about the speed of a car on the highway. The fastest humans can run only 28 miles per hour (45 kmh). However, a human can beat a cheetah in a race. How? If it's a marathon! Cheetahs can only sustain their speed for short bursts. Meanwhile, humans were built to run at an average speed for a long time. So if the race is 26 feet (8 m), the cheetah will win. If the race is 26 miles (42 km), the human will win.

MORE ON RUNNING

Humans may be the best endurance runners on the planet. Some super athletes are able to run 100 miles (161 km) in a single race. Why would this be important in our evolution? When chasing a potential meal—one we couldn't outrun—we couldn't keep up with them as they ran away. Instead, we kept running, and eventually caught up to them when they were tired and weak.

NO. 35
GERMY KISSES

Your body's immune system is really good at fighting germs that could make you sick. While newborn babies don't have fully developed immune systems, there is something that protects them from germs: their mother's kisses! When a mother kisses her baby, her body gets a sample of whatever germs are on the baby. Her immune system analyzes for bad germs, and then produces breast milk for the baby that will kill the bad germs.

CLEAN THOSE BINKIES

Have you ever seen a baby drop a pacifier, and Mom puts it in her mouth to clean it before giving it back? It sounds gross and unhealthy, but a scientific study reports that this may help babies avoid allergies later in life. The study says the germs the mother gives her baby help develop the immune system.

NO. 36
TONGUE POWER

Your tongue is always working, even when you're sleeping. It helps with eating, swallowing, talking, cleaning your teeth, filtering out germs, and more. And unlike other muscles, it never gets tired (which is why a chatty friend or sibling can talk for hours!). The tongue is actually a boneless group of eight intertwined muscles. These muscles work together to create superior strength and flexibility—much like an elephant's trunk. Your tongue may not be able to lift a tree out of the ground, but for its size, it's plenty strong!

MORE ABOUT TONGUES

Human tongues have between 2,000 and 4,000 taste buds, which can taste sweet, sour, salty, and bitter foods. There's a fifth flavor we can sense, called *umami*, which is described as a pleasant savory flavor that is found in fermented foods, cheeses, mushrooms, tomatoes, and some slow-cooked foods.

NO. 37
WATERWORKS

Of all the amazingly weird things our bodies do, crying is perhaps the most mysterious. Babies cry to get their parents' attention, and all animals produce tears to lubricate their eyes. But as far as we know, humans are the only animals that cry emotional tears. That means we cry when we're hurt, sad, happy, exhausted, angry, and surprised. And scientists aren't quite sure why. Some say it makes us feel better by releasing emotional tension. Others believe it is a signal that we need help or comfort. A few scientists even believe crying removes harmful chemicals, which then makes us feel better.

MORE ABOUT TEARS

Tears are composed of oil, water, and mucus. The water contains sodium, proteins, and other substances. The oil slows evaporation. Some of your tears end up falling through tiny openings in the eyelid and end up in your nasal cavity. That's why you get all stuffed up when you cry.

NO. 38
GONE RED

You thought it would be nice to give the girl next door a flower. She's so happy and thankful that she gives you a kiss on the cheek. You can't see them, but you know your cheeks are turning redder than a bushel of apples. You're blushing. This happens to lots of people when they feel embarrassed and self-conscious. Nobody's really sure why we blush. And nobody really likes blushing as it usually just leads to more embarrassment! But there's no stopping it.

MORE ON BLUSHING

You can blame adrenaline for your red cheeks. (See "Super Strength & Speed" on page 15.) As adrenaline prepares you to face a fear (such as being singled out by a teacher or being noticed by a cute boy or girl), your blood vessels dilate, or expand, causing more blood to flow to your cheeks.

NO. 39
STOMACH SOUP

The food we eat goes through a multi-step process known as *digestion*. Once you chew and swallow, the food bits end up in your stomach. The gastric juices in your stomach further break down the food. Part of this liquid is an extremely powerful chemical called *hydrochloric acid*. This stuff is so powerful that it is used to remove rust from steel and is an ingredient in toilet bowl cleaners. A drop of it on a wooden tabletop would eat right through it. The acid in our guts not only helps digest our food, but it also kills harmful bacteria that we swallow.

MORE ON STOMACH JUICE

So why doesn't the acid just eat through our stomach? Well, it tries! The stomach lining, however, creates a new, thick coating of mucus every few days in order to keep the acid from hurting us. When some of this acid gets past our defenses, we can get heartburn, which is really acid going up into the esophagus.

NO. 40
SWIMMING IN SALIVA

Spit. Spittle, Dribble. Drool. Slobber. There are lots of funny words for the liquid in your mouth, but the official word is *saliva*. And without it, you couldn't taste, swallow, or digest your food. Saliva also protects your teeth from cavities and your gums from disease. Spit even helps wounds in your mouth heal quickly and prevents bad breath! There are six *glands*, or organs that release chemicals for different purposes, in your head that produce up to half a gallon (4L) of saliva a day. In a lifetime, that's enough to fill up a decent-sized swimming pool!

MORE ABOUT SALIVA

A cut in your mouth heals faster than one elsewhere because saliva has special cells and proteins that work to clean and mend. But it only works on cuts inside your mouth. If you lick a cut on your body, you could infect it because your saliva is also full of bacteria.

NO. 41
OPEN WIDE

You have been yawning since before you were born. You yawn when you wake up in the morning and before you go to bed at night. You yawn when you're tired or bored—even when you try not to. So why do we yawn? Scientists believe that yawning helps to cool down our brains to help us think a little more clearly. Yawning increases heart rate and blood flow while delivering a gulp of air—all of which cool the blood around your brain.

MORE ABOUT YAWNS

Up to 60 percent of humans will yawn if they see or hear someone else yawn, read about yawning, or simply think about yawning. Nobody knows for sure why yawns are contagious, but the next time you're in a crowded room, yawn and look around to see if you created a yawn epidemic.

NO. 42
HEAD SPIN

Spin yourself around quickly five to ten times. Then stop. You should feel a little dizzy. This is called *vertigo*, and it happens whenever the part of your inner ear that senses motion sends the wrong signal to your brain. When you stop spinning, the inner ear still thinks you're moving and tells the brain that. This causes dizziness. Vertigo can happen on roller coasters and merry-go-rounds or even when you stand up suddenly.

NOT SO DIZZY

How do spinning dancers avoid dizziness? When they spin, they keep their eyes fixed on one point and whip their heads around quickly to that point during each spin. This tricks their bodies into thinking they are standing still.

NO. 43
BE FLEXIBLE

How far can you bend over? You don't have to be double jointed (see page 7) to be flexible. People with perfectly normal amounts of flexibility can do the splits, bend over backward, hold their leg straight up in the air, and more. Cheerleaders, dancers, and gymnasts work hard to increase their flexibility so they can do these tricks safely without hurting themselves. Becoming more flexible takes practice and patience. Yoga, Pilates, and ballet all help with becoming more flexible, as do certain exercises.

MORE ON FLEXIBILITY

Stretching exercises help increase flexibility, but not in the way that you think. Your muscles and joints don't get longer. Instead, scientists believe stretching gets your nervous system used to the muscle extensions so that over time, it stops sending pain signals to the brain.

NO. 44
UPSIDE-DOWN EATING

The very idea of hanging upside down and eating seems impossible. Won't food stay in your throat until you stand right-side up? Food doesn't just drop down your throat into your stomach. It's pushed toward the stomach through the *esophagus*, a tube connecting your mouth to your stomach. When you eat or drink, the smooth muscles of the esophagus contract, or tighten, which pushes the food and liquid down. Once the food reaches the end of the esophagus, a valve called the *sphincter* closes so the food stays there. This process is stronger than gravity, which is why you can eat upside down.

THE WRONG PIPE

Sometimes after eating or drinking, it feels like our food went down the wrong pipe. This happens when instead of entering the esophagus, our food enters the *trachea*. This "pipe" is for breathing, and it's usually closed when you eat. However, if you're distracted or eating too quickly, food or liquid can end up in here, causing violent coughing and possibly choking.

NO. 45
USING YOUR HEAD

In many cultures around the world, people carry and balance heavy loads on their heads without pain. This practice goes back thousands of years. Scientists studying head-loading believe a 100-pound person (45 kg) can carry 20 pounds (9 kg) on his or her head without needing any extra energy. And people with years of practice can carry up to 70 percent of their body weight on their head.

MORE ON HEAD-LOADING

You cannot just start carrying all your school textbooks on your head. Head-loading takes years of practice and conditioning. Young girls in East Africa and other developing nations begin carrying small items on their heads when they are young and slowly build their neck muscles as they carry heavier and heavier items. So start small and practice!

NO. 46
FORCEFUL FINGERS

The muscles that move your fingers are super strong. They help your fingers grip and lift heavy objects. They can support your weight while you do fingertip push-ups (with some training, of course). They help rock climbers cling to small ledges while climbing the side of a cliff. And for some extreme bodybuilders, one finger can lift up to 500 pounds (227 kg)! That's a lot of power from ten fairly small body parts that don't even have any muscles of their own!

MORE ON FINGERS

That's right! Your fingers don't have any muscles. The muscles that operate your fingers are in your palms and forearms. You can see the tendons that deliver motion from your forearm muscles to your fingers. Stretch out an arm and wiggle your fingers or clench your fist. Can you see the tendons moving under your skin at the wrist, forearm, and back of your hand?

NO. 47
GOING BATTY

Echolocation is the ability to use sound instead of sight to sense your surroundings. Making a noise creates sound waves. The sound waves bounce off nearby objects and make their way back to the brain to help create a picture of your surroundings. Animals such as bats, a few birds, whales, and dolphins use echolocation to navigate and find their dinner. Humans can teach themselves echolocation as well. For instance, blind people sometimes tap with a cane or click with their tongue to navigate their environment.

MORE ON ECHOLOCATION

Humans aren't born knowing how to echolocate; however, even sighted individuals can teach themselves to see without using their eyes. Daniel Kish, who has been blind since he was one year old, uses echolocation to hike, mountain bike, and more. He's known as the real-life Batman.

NO. 48
THE EYES HAVE IT

If someone shines a light in your eyes, your *pupils*, or the black middle part of your eyes, will shrink. Take the light away, and your pupil will expand, or dilate. Light is not the only thing that will get your pupils moving, however. If presented with something pleasing, your pupils will dilate to nearly twice their normal size. Ice cream, a cupcake, a bouquet of beautiful flowers, a new baseball mitt...all these things will make your eyes go wide if you like them. And who doesn't like cupcakes!?

MORE ABOUT PUPILS

Scientists have discovered that people with dilated pupils are considered more attractive than those with smaller pupils. That's why babies' eyes dilate when looking at adults and why toys and anime characters have really big eyes and pupils—to draw our attention.

NO. 49
LOOKING CROSS

Just about everyone has heard that if you cross your eyes they can get stuck that way! But this is not true at all. In fact, your eyes cross naturally any time you focus on something up close. Crossing your eyes on purpose simply means you're telling your eye muscles to move inward at the same time. Try this: hold a pencil in front of your face at arm's length. Slowly bring it toward your nose. As your eyes track the pencil, they move inward and cross. And at some point, you will probably see two pencils (or two caterpillars, if that's what is right in front of your face!).

MORE ON MOVING YOUR EYES

With practice, some people can move one eye independently of the other. (That's when one eye moves and the other doesn't.) It's weird-looking and a great party trick, and it's not harmful.

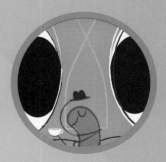

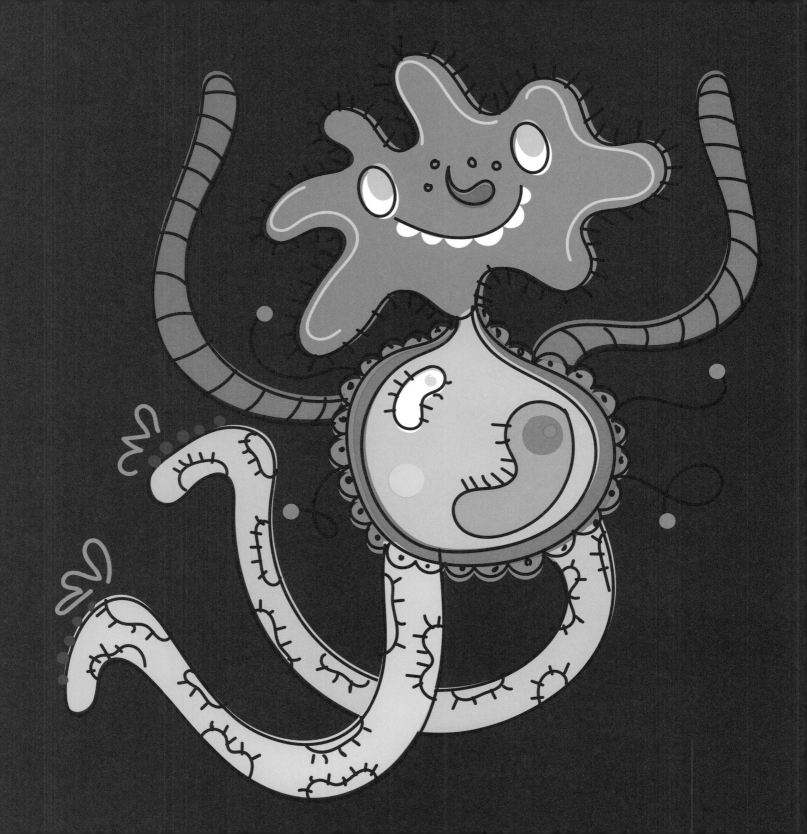

NO. 50
YOUR BODY IS A PLANET

Your body is an amazing place to live. Just ask the trillions of bacteria, viruses, and other microorganisms that call your body home. A large portion of the cells in your body are not human—they are *microbes*, or tiny microorganisms too small to see without a microscope. They live everywhere in us: our stomachs, mouths, noses, blood, hair, elbows, and more. While some of these microbes can make us sick, most of them help us digest our food, protect us from disease, keep us healthy, and eat other microbes. These microbes need our body to live, and our body needs these microbes.

A MITE-Y EXISTENCE

One such microbe that lives on us is called *Demodex folliculorum*. These are eight-legged, spiderlike creatures that live their entire lives on our faces. That's right, you have tiny spiders on your face! Scientists aren't sure why they live on us, but they are harmless.

Also in this series

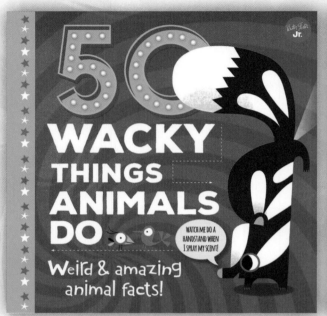

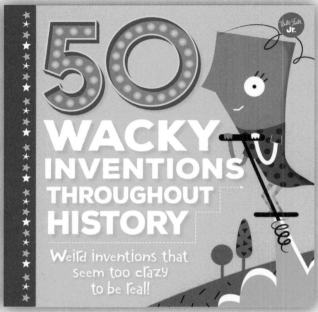

50 Wacky Things Animals Do describes 50 peculiar animal behaviors that seem too crazy to be true—but are!

50 Wacky Inventions Throughout History describes 50 weird, silly, and mind-boggling inventions.